Power

MW01223755

How to Use Your Mind to Succeed in Life and Work:
Tricks to Overcome Your Self-Doubt and Achieve Success.
(VOL 1)

Amoo O. Olaleye

1

Table of Contents

Preface

Never underestimate the power of using your mind. It's one of the best tools you have for success.

This book is about how to use your mind to be successful in life and work. It is not a how-to book on meditation, but rather a book on the power of your mind. This book is about how to use your mind to be successful in life and work.

This book will give you the mental tools you need to achieve all your goals, no matter how big or small they may be. How to Use Your Mind to Achieve Greater Success in Life and Work!

Your mind is what makes you. It is what you use to think, remember, decide, create, imagine, and feel. Your mind is the most important tool you have in life. It is truly the most powerful tool you have. It's one of the main reasons you are here reading this guide. Your mind is what got you interested in this book; it is what will keep you coming back for more. What you will learn in this book:

- How to use your mind to get yourself out of any situation, even if that situation is in your own mind.

- How to use your mind to instantly increase your self-esteem.

- How to use your mind to achieve virtually anything you can think of.

- How to use your mind to become a "super-human" being.

Some parts of this book contain the core principles you must understand in order to use your mind effectively. These are the bedrock basics you must learn if you ever want to use your mind to be more successful in life and work. Another section of this book is where all the magic happens. It is here that you will learn specific techniques you can use to put these principles into action in your daily life. Throughout this entire book, I will be giving you tools, techniques, hints, and insider secrets on how to use your mind to be more successful. I am going to give you an incredible number of instructions to chew on. You won't be able to stop thinking about what you are going to learn in this book! This book was written for everyone. No matter who you are, what you do for a living, or how much money you make.

INTRODUCTION

In today's competitive environment, it's easy to underestimate the power of our minds, which is why a single bad review can be enough to ruin a reputation and make a business seem unreliable, so you need to be aware of what people are thinking about you.

You will never reach a place of total peace and contentment in this life until you learn to accept the things you cannot change and simply move on.

The first step in this process is to become aware of the things you can change... and then, to stop obsessing about them. This is not an easy thing for most people to do. It's much easier to dwell on what's wrong with your life than it is to simply accept it as it is.

One of the most important lessons is that our minds are much more powerful than we give them credit for. Most people never learn this lesson because they don't know any better. They get an education that teaches them only a small part of what their mind is capable of learning. They get an education that makes them "cognitive cripples," unable to think outside the box. These people will be perfectly happy living in the world as it is today, with all its problems.

It is not the strongest of the species that survives, nor the most intelligent. It is the one that is most responsive to change. A short time ago, a group of scientists proved that what you focus on expands. They did this by having a group of people stare at a dot for two hours per day, five days per week, for a period of eleven weeks. Then, they measured the size of their "focus pool" and found it to be much larger than expected. In fact, it was more than 2,000% bigger! What does this mean? Simply put, what you focus on expands.

This discovery is huge because it proves that we are all capable of changing our focus, as long as we are aware that what we focus on expands. It also means that we can control where we focus. If you have ever played the games Concentration or Tetris, then you know that what you focus on will grow. It's similar to how a person playing an instrument will eventually develop muscle memory for a particular note or scale. The question now becomes: how do you focus?

Well, to tell you the truth, I don't know exactly how to focus. However, I do know that whenever I start to get stressed out, my ability to focus seems to diminish. And, whenever I take some time off, my ability to focus seems to improve. In other words, when my stress levels are high, I am less able to focus, and when my stress levels are low, I am more able to focus. It appears to me that the best way to get into the "groove" of becoming more focused is to do something physical, like exercise or working on a puzzle. Another thing you can do to improve your focus is to learn to meditate. There are many different types of meditation. But, in general, most forms of meditation reduce your overall stress level. This means that you will be able to focus better. Here's another little-known fact: the human eye can see about 1/10th of one percent (0.01%) of what it sees.

In Power of the Mind, Amoo O. Olaleye explains that the brain has many parts that interact with each other. From the earliest of times, people have known that certain mental techniques could help us improve our lives—and they've used the power of the mind to enhance their lives and to become better leaders. It's amazing what a little knowledge can do.

For example, do you know that the world's best salesmen are not born, but rather, they are made? It's true. The real masters of closing the deal are those who know the art and science of brainwashing. They have the ability to program the minds of their prospects so that they will buy from them without even realizing it. One way to do this is by using a strong "engineered" emotion.

This is one of the most powerful ways to close the sale. A brain is a wonderful machine, but it's not perfect. It can be influenced by external factors, and one of the most important is your state of mind. So, if you want to change how you think about something or how you feel about it, then you have to train your brain to think or feel in a new way. And that's exactly what we're going to do in this book.

CHAPTER 1

How To Use Your Mind To Change The World

How can we use our minds to change the world? This is one of the most important questions in the world. The first step is to take a look at yourself and think about how it works. It may seem impossible to change your mind, but it is possible if you really want to. All we have to do is use the power of our minds to help us achieve our goals. The first thing you should realize is that you are not your mind. You have a body and a brain, but they don't exist independently of your mind. Your body and your brain work together to keep you alive. Your mind also plays an important role in keeping your body functioning properly. It keeps everything running smoothly and helps you make important decisions. You can't make progress without using your mind. The next thing that you have to realize is that your mind can be used for good or bad purposes. The power of the mind comes from your thoughts, which are what you think about, whether they are positive or negative. You can use your thoughts to make something happen or to stop something from happening. So, if you want to change your life for the better, you need to use your thoughts to achieve that goal. Your mind is the most powerful tool that you have, and it should be used wisely to make the changes that you want.

Many people have great minds and they use them for good. However, most people have poor minds and they use them for bad purposes. It is up to each of us to develop our minds and to use them for good. To help you develop your mind, here are some tips:

- **Reading Books:** The best way to learn anything is to read about it. Read books on history, biographies, how to improve your health, psychology, success secrets, etc. Read at least one book every month. Don't worry if the book isn't related to your field of interest. Just read it anyway. You'll get ideas from other areas of interest. This will help you develop your mind.

- **Watch Tapes:** If you are interested in a certain subject, you should watch some of the best speakers on that subject. This will help you learn by doing. The more you do, the better you'll become. Watch educational, motivational, and inspirational tapes. Do this at least once a month.

- **Listen to Audio Books:** There are many good books that have accompanying audio tapes. These books have experienced people reading the stories and telling what's in them. It's a good way to get information without having to struggle to read it. You can do this at home with your MP.

Many people spend a lot of time thinking about ways to improve their lives. However, not enough time is spent thinking about how to make the world a better place. Sometimes, when I give speeches, I tell the audience that they should devote at least as much time as they do to improving their own lives to making the world a better place. This is not a new idea. Many great men and women have believed this. Gandhi spent almost all of his time thinking about how to improve the lives of the people of India. Martin Luther King Jr. was very concerned with making the United States a better place. Bill Gates has given more of his money to help people than any other human being in history. These people, and many others like them, believed that the only way to make the world a better place was to change individual lives for the better. This is true. However, we also need to change the world by changing the way it is organized. We need to organize it in such a way that benefits everybody, instead of just a few people. This is not an easy thing to do. Most of the time, those who run the world are extremely selfish. They only care about themselves and their own self-interest.

What you think about becomes a reality. If you think you are not good at something, you will almost certainly prove yourself to be not good at it. Your confidence is your greatest asset because it will get you to the top and hold you there. If you want to be successful, you have to believe that you can succeed. No one else will do it for you. You have to be the one who believes in yourself.

It's all about confidence. It's the most important thing in life because if you don't have confidence, you won't be able to do anything. There is no way to get anywhere in life without self-confidence. If you have confidence, you can get through anything. If you don't have confidence, you can't get through anything.

The thing I have learned about success is that it takes a lot of hard work and dedication. The hard part is putting in the time and doing the work. The easy part is getting the reward. Success is not about what you know; it's about who you know. The more people you know, the better your life will be. You can't achieve anything if you are always surrounded by losers. What you think about becomes a reality. If you think you are not good at something, you will almost certainly prove yourself to be not good at it. Your confidence is your greatest asset because it will get you to the top and hold you there.

A collection of interviews with top world-class athletes, each edited together by their mental coach, Louie Anderson, to show how they think about performance. We are living in a world where it's all about results, and people are judged on the results they achieve. But as Louie Anderson has written, "Results are only meaningful when you know why you are doing what you are doing. If you don't understand your own process, then you'll never be able to understand the results.

You have to know what you are doing if you want to do better, because it's just a little bit of knowledge. If you truly desire to be the best, then you have to know what the best are doing. You see, if you truly want to be the best, then you have to keep on learning and improving, and that requires... knowledge of what the best are doing!

Knowledge is power. However, not just any kind of knowledge will do. You see, if you just learn anything, no matter how pertinent or useful, it will be wasted on you! You see, you have to learn what the very top people in your field are doing if you really want to be the best. How do you find out what the best people in your field are doing? It's actually quite simple. All you have to do is pay attention to what they are saying and read, watch, and copy. Hey, that sounds like fun, doesn't it? Well, it is if you know what you are doing.

Using your mind to change the world is easier than you think. It's a lot like riding a bicycle. Once you learn how to ride a bike, you will never forget it. If you want to change the world, you must first change your mind. There are ten critical steps to follow if you want to become a master of mind control:

First, you have to learn how to control your own mind. This is the most important step in the process. If you are not able to control your own mind, then it will be very difficult for you to control anyone else's mind. You can start controlling your mind by simply telling yourself that you are going to make a habit of thinking positively all the time and that you will not allow negative thoughts to take over your mind.

If you think that your mind has become so bad that it is not possible for you to change it, then you are wrong. It is true that your mind is what defines you and that you cannot change it, but you can control it. Control your mind by following these simple steps:

- Always be aware of your mind. You should always be aware of what is happening in your mind and what is happening outside your mind.

- When you are aware of your mind, you should not allow your mind to do anything except help you achieve your goals.

- Your first goal is to learn to think positively. If you think negatively all the time, it will be difficult for you to change to a positive way of thinking.

Therefore, your first job is to eliminate as much negative thinking as you can from your mental programming.

- Learn to think creatively. To do this, you must get out of your own little box and think about other people's boxes.

- You should always be on the lookout for new ways to solve problems and achieve goals.

- Learn to think analytically. To do this, you must break down complex issues into their simplest components. You should strive to understand all aspects of a problem before you decide what to do. Also, you should analyze solutions and choices in order to make the best decision.

- Learn to think prospectively. To do this, you should constantly be thinking about the future and planning for it.

- Learn to think contractually. This means that you should always be thinking about legal matters and the obligations that you have to other people.

- Learn to think relationally. You should think about your relationships with other people and how to improve them.

- Learn to think logistically. You should be thinking about all of the things that need to be done in order for you to reach your goals.

- Learn to think operationally. When you think operationally, you should be thinking about how to actually get the things you want.

Second, you must practice controlling your mind over and over again until you have mastered it, simply by observing your thoughts without getting involved in them.

If a negative thought occurs to you, just acknowledge it by saying something like, "Hmm, that's a negative thought." If a positive thought occurs to you, say something like, "Hmn, that's a positive thought. I will be happy. " This technique of simply observing your thoughts is the key to the method of controlling your mind. This may sound difficult at first, but if you stick with it, it will get easier and easier. In addition, you will find that you are not as bothered by the negative thoughts that occur to you as before. You will also find that you can think about things you want to do or that you would like to experience more frequently.

Third, you must have the patience to be patient with yourself, to keep practicing until you have achieved success. It is not enough to simply read a book and then expect to get good at writing. Not at all.The only way to get good at anything is through practice. And, in this case, that means sticking to it until you become proficient. If you want to be a world-class at anything, you must do what all great people do: work hard!

Fourth, you must practice the technique you've learned in a quiet place where there are no distractions. If you can't do that, then it's not for you. "Practice" So now that you have your first basic skill, it's time to get down to business and learn how to use it. As you practice, you will notice a pattern emerging. You'll see a series of moves that seem similar but somehow different from one another. This is because you are using a different part of the brain to perform each move. Now that you know how to move your head, it's time to learn how to use it. If you want to play tennis, you need to be able to swing the racket in order to hit the ball. If you want to play chess, you need to be able to move your hand in order to make your next move. And if you want to read a book, you need to move your eyes in order to see the words on the page.

Fifth, you must keep practicing the techniques for at least a month in order to build up sufficient energy so that you can make the leap into your subconscious mind.

- Consider this when you are learning something new, it is important to remember and internalize what you have learned. This is especially important with meditation and hypnosis because you will need to be able to remember how to use the techniques once you start practicing them on a regular basis. To help you remember, I suggest you get a friend to help you keep a journal and ask him or her to remind you to meditate every day and to use positive suggestions and affirmations every day.

- Give Yourself Permission To Be A Human Being Again! Don't try to change into a robot or be someone you're not. You were born an individual, and you have the right to be you. Don't suppress your feelings, thoughts, or desires just because they are not "the correct ones." You don't have to buy into the propaganda of advertising or the BS stories being told to you by the media. You are unique.

Sixth, you must learn how to visualize the things you want and then put those things into action by taking specific actions. Visualization is one of the most powerful tools in the world, but it will not do you any good unless you act on what you have visualized. For example, I have often told people that if they visualized themselves driving a race car at speeds of up to 180 miles per hour, they would become nervous. They would then go out and drive their cars at speeds of up to 60 miles per hour and experience no fear or anxiety. The reason for this is that they are only visualizing the speed and not actually doing it. It is important to visualize what you want, but then it must be translated into action. Finally, you must learn how to trust yourself and your intuition. There is a saying in Japan that translates as "If you want to know the truth, look inside yourself." This means that the only person who can tell you the truth about yourself is yourself.

Seventh, you must have faith that what you want is achievable, even if you don't know how you will achieve it yet. This was the hardest one for me to embrace because I felt so much pressure to be good at everything and to be perfect in every aspect of my life. But I had to realize that I could choose to live my life by the principles of this book rather than try to be perfect all the time.

Eighth, you must have the courage to pursue your goals no matter what others may think of them. And you must have the courage to admit when you are wrong. It is only by admitting our mistakes that we can move on to greater success. The main point I am trying to make is this: failure is not an option! You see, if you truly believe that failure is not an option, then all sorts of other options become available to you.

Ninth, you must make yourself a promise to never give up, to continue to try and to persevere until you achieve your goal. That's what the people who have been successful did; they didn't give up, even when all the odds were against them. You know, I don't think any of us are ever going to stop trying to sell our ideas and our products. We can't. It's in our bones. It's in our blood. But we can stop making excuses for not selling. We CAN stop saying things like "Oh, it's too hard" or "The market is saturated" or "Nobody wants what I'm selling." No! No! No! Those are the very thoughts that keep us from ever getting anywhere! Those are the thoughts that prevent us from achieving our goals.

Tenth, you must have the wisdom to know when to stop struggling and accepting defeat, and instead, start finding ways to make your goal easier to achieve. Finally, you must know this: the process of changing your life for the better is not a straight-line path. It is more like a mountain range with many valleys and dead ends. You will constantly be confronted with new challenges and problems that will seem to block your progress. But, don't despair. Just keep forging ahead until you reach the top of the next mountain. Then, take a breather and enjoy the view. And keep going. The journey is as important as the destination.

Improve Your Mind With Meditation.

Some people think that life is hard. They see the world as a place where they can't succeed. They get discouraged and give up trying. Others see life as a wonderful place.

They see a lot of opportunities and believe that they can do anything. The truth is that no one should give up because they have challenges in their lives. We all have to face challenges at some point in our lives. What's important is that we overcome them and get better at life. Life is full of challenges, but if you work hard, you will succeed. Life is full of opportunities, and it's up to you to seize the moment and seize success. When you face challenges, try to look on the bright side of things. If you are having problems, ask for help. Don't worry about what other people think.

You can change your mind and even your whole world. You can become a different person and get rid of all the problems in your life. You can do this by using your mind. For instance, if you want to have better relationships, then you should learn how to be happy. It is possible to be happy all the time. It's about your mindset. You should try to learn how to be happy. You'll be more focused and happier when you do that. It can be very hard to believe in yourself, let alone make the leap to actually act on your convictions. This is where meditation comes into play. Meditation is a key part of many religions and Eastern spiritual practices, but there are secular benefits to meditation too. It helps with the decision-making process and can help improve our lives in a wide variety of ways.

How to meditate There are many different types of meditation. Each type will have a slightly different effect on you. Some meditation types include:

Mindfulness Meditation:- This type of meditation focuses on being present in the moment and noticing the small things that you experience. It is based on the ancient Buddhist concept of "mindfulness" and is designed to improve your mental and emotional well-being.

It has been proven to help with stress, anxiety, depression, and other conditions. The key is to focus on what you are experiencing right now, rather than worrying about what might happen in the future. It is important to practice this type of meditation regularly because it can be difficult to stay focused for long periods of time.

Breathing Meditation: – This type of meditation helps you slow down and become more aware of your breathing. The idea is to breathe in slowly and deeply, hold the breath for a moment, and then breathe out slowly and deeply. This is known as mindfulness meditation. You can also do this type of meditation with your eyes closed or while listening to music, which will help you focus on your breathing. The key to successful meditation is learning to be aware of your breath without judgment.

Relaxation: In this type of meditation, you learn to slow down your breathing and tense muscles until you reach a calm, relaxed state.

This is known as the "alert" stage of meditation. In the "relaxed" stage, your mind is clear and open, and you can begin to focus on your object of meditation. This is also known as the "concentration" or "focus" stage of meditation. Here are some tips on how to do this:

- Start by sitting in a comfortable position with your back straight and your hands in a comfortable position.

- Take several deep breaths in and out of your nose. Once you are breathing normally, start counting backwards from 100 to 1. When you reach 1, stop breathing and concentrate on the sound of your breath going in and out of your nose. Count slowly for about 10 seconds, and then count slowly for 10 seconds again.

Repeat these steps until you reach the number 10. When you reach the number 10, stop counting and take one more deep breath in and out of your nose. Take a deep breath in and then exhale very slowly. Count to 10 and then stop counting. Take another deep breath in and exhale slowly. Count to 10 and then stop counting. Continue this exercise for about 5 minutes. Then, when you are ready, close your eyes and begin concentrating on the object of meditation: your breathing. You can do this for as long as you want. If you have trouble focusing on your breathing, simply follow the steps above but count backwards from 100 to 1, then count from 1 to 2, and so on. You can use this method to focus on any object of meditation. Once you are comfortable with this technique, you can start practicing the "concentration" or "focus" stage of meditation. You can practice this stage of meditation anytime, but it is especially helpful to practice it before bedtime.

Chill Out: This type of meditation is great for beginners because it is simple and easy to do.

Reflection Meditation: – This type of meditation is focused on thinking about the past or the future, allowing your mind to wander. As you do this, simply observe and acknowledge whatever thoughts or images arise in your mind. Do not try to control or direct your thoughts in any way. Just keep an eye out for them as they happen. When you are done, simply return to your breath and begin the cycle again.

Thinking Meditation:– This type of meditation is focused on trying to understand yourself or the world around you. Here are some questions you might ask yourself when doing this type of meditation. What is my goal? What do I most need to learn? What is my deepest fear? What am I most passionate about? What do I most want to become a reality? What is my strongest suit?

What is my special gift that I could give to the world?

Summary

It may seem impossible to change your mind, but it is possible if you really want to. All we have to do is use the power of our minds to help us achieve our goals. Your mind is the most powerful tool that you have, and it should be used wisely. Many people spend a lot of time thinking about ways to improve their lives. Not enough time is spent thinking about how to make the world a better place.

If you want to be successful, you have to believe that you can succeed. You have to be the one who believes in yourself. Confidence is the most important thing in life. If you don't have confidence, you won't be able to do anything. Success is not about what you know; it's about who you know.

The more people you know, the better your life will be. If you want to change the world, you must first change your mind. There are ten steps to becoming a master of mind control. First, you have to learn how to control your own mind. Then, you need to eliminate as much negative thinking as you can from your brain.

You should always be on the lookout for new ways to solve problems and achieve goals. When you think operationally, you should be thinking about how to get the things you want. You must practice controlling your mind over and over again until you have mastered it. If you want to be world-class at anything, you must do what all great people do: work hard! You must practice the technique you've learned in a quiet place where there are no distractions.

If you can't do that, then it's not for you. Don't suppress your feelings, thoughts, or desires just because they are not "the correct ones". Don't buy into the propaganda of advertising or the BS stories being told to you by the media. Have faith that what you want is achievable, even if you don't know how to achieve it yet. You must have the courage to pursue your goals, no matter what others may think.

You must know when to stop struggling and accepting defeat, and instead, start finding ways to make your goal easier to achieve. The process of changing your life is not a straight-line path, but rather a mountain range with many valleys and dead ends. There are many different types of meditation. Each type will have a slightly different effect on you. Meditation is a key part of many religions and Eastern spiritual practices.

There are secular benefits to meditation too. It helps with the decision-making process and can improve our lives in a variety of ways. Meditation has been proven to help with stress, anxiety, depression, and other conditions. The key is to focus on what you are experiencing right now, rather than worrying about the future. Here are some tips on how to get into a more relaxed state of meditation.

When you are ready, close your eyes and start concentrating on the object of meditation: your breathing. Count backwards from 100 to 1, then count from 1 to 2, and so on. This type of meditation is great for beginners because it is simple and easy to do.

CHAPTER 2:

8 Mindfulness Tips to Boost Your Happiness

We all want to be happy. But we also need to learn how to be happier. Research indicates that there are many different ways to boost our happiness. One way to do this is through mindfulness. In fact, recent research suggests that people who practice mindfulness may even experience happiness benefits for years to come.

Mindfulness is the practice of being aware of your present circumstances without judgment. It's the act of paying attention in a non-judgmental way to whatever is happening here and now. It is essentially awareness training for your brain. You can learn to be more mindful by paying attention to the things you do on a daily basis, such as eating, brushing your teeth, driving a car, walking down the street, or talking with a friend. Being mindful is like exercising your brain. The more you do it, the easier it will get.

As your mindfulness practice grows, you may find yourself noticing more of your surroundings, noticing your thoughts, and noticing how you respond to situations. You may notice that you are less reactive to others and events around you. Your sense of self may expand and you may become more accepting of others and yourself. This is the beauty of mindfulness. It works for all of us, not just "special people." Mindfulness is a skill that can be applied to many different aspects of your life. It can help you with your relationships, your work, your health, and your happiness. You can learn to be mindful through meditation and/or by paying attention to your daily activities. Here are six ways to become more mindful:

Notice your thoughts.

When you notice your thoughts, you are training your brain to focus on what is happening right now. You can practice noticing your thoughts by doing something simple, such as eating. When you are about to eat, think about what you are about to eat. If you are thinking about all of the things that could go wrong while you are eating, this is a bad habit to break. Try to pay attention only to what you are actually eating. You can also notice your thoughts when you are driving or talking to a friend. This is helpful because when you pay attention to your thoughts, you are training your brain to be more aware of the present moment.

This exercise is very powerful because it will help you gain control over your thoughts. You may have been thinking about a stressful situation for so long that your mind has become very habitual. If you start paying attention to your thoughts now, you will see that you are just becoming accustomed to them. You will start to notice that your mind is running in the past and future. When you notice your thoughts, you will learn to stop and focus on the present. To practice noticing your thoughts, start by sitting quietly for five minutes. Then think of something that is happening right now, such as the sound of a bird singing. As you sit there, notice everything that you can notice about what you are experiencing. Notice how your body feels, what you can smell, what you can hear, and what you can taste. After five minutes, move on to noticing your thoughts.

You can also practice noticing your thoughts in other ways. For example, you can try to notice what you are thinking as you drive down the street. This will help you stay focused on the present moment. You can also practice noticing your thoughts while you are talking to someone. This will help you to stop thinking about the past or the future. It will also help you listen to what the other person is saying. You can practice noticing your thoughts when you are reading, playing a game, or taking a walk.

When you are feeling upset, it is easy to get lost in your emotions. You may feel like you are losing control of your life. When you are feeling upset, your mind is not thinking clearly. It is just running in the past and the future. The more upset you get, the worse your thoughts become. It is helpful to be aware of what you are thinking so that you can learn to control your thoughts. When you are upset, it is difficult to think clearly, and this makes it very hard to learn anything new. You can practice dealing with your emotions by doing something simple, such as eating, as I mentioned above. When you are upset, it is easy to overeat. You may find that when you are upset, you eat more than you normally eat. When you eat, try to focus on what you are actually eating. If you are upset about something that happened in the past, try to think about what you are going to eat right now. You may want to eat a salad or fruit. This will help you take care of yourself. You can also practice noticing your emotions when you are eating. When you are upset, it is easy to get lost in your thoughts. Try to pay attention only to what you are actually eating. When you are feeling upset, it is helpful to notice what you are thinking about. You can do this by practicing noticing your thoughts when you are feeling upset. If you are thinking about an upsetting situation in the past, notice what you are thinking about.

Emotional Intelligence

Sometimes we don't realize how much we are thinking about the past or worrying about the future. We tend to think in a linear fashion, from the present to the past and into the future. This means that we are not thinking about the present moment, which is what mindfulness is all about. To practice mindfulness, you need to become aware of your thoughts, feelings, and emotions. But you also need to train your brain to pay attention to the present moment. To do this, take time to reflect on your day. For example, you could write down your thoughts and feelings on a piece of paper or simply ask yourself how you are feeling. When you are finished writing, read through the paper and see if there is anything that stands out to you. This will help you recognize patterns in your thinking.

Once you identify these patterns, you can make an effort to change them. For example, you might think, "I always feel bad when I don't get my work done on time." Then, you can think, "I am going to make an effort to be more organized." Or, "I am going to make sure I get everything done so that I won't have to worry about it anymore." You may also find that certain emotions or thoughts come up over and over again. These are the thoughts and emotions that are connected to your past and future. To deal with these emotions, you need to stop and take some time to reflect on what happened in the past and what might happen in the future. A lot of the time, we are not aware of our emotions and feelings. It is important to learn how to identify them. This is called emotional intelligence. This is because if you don't know how to identify them, you cannot understand how they affect you. You also can't understand why you act in certain ways.

Practice Mindful Breathing.

Mindful breathing is an ancient meditation practice that can be used to help increase your overall sense of well-being. If you've never practiced mindfulness meditation before, this would be a good place to start. As soon as you notice your mind wandering off into the future or the past, gently bring it back to the present moment and notice the sensations in your body. You may also notice that your mind has thoughts or images that come and go without your permission. When these thoughts occur, acknowledge them and then return to the breath. This is how you learn to control your thoughts. You may find that you can notice your thoughts without becoming overwhelmed by them.

Over time, you will learn to watch your thoughts arise, acknowledge them, and then return to the breath. It takes practice, but it is very easy to learn. As you continue to practice mindful breathing, you may notice that your thoughts slow down and your focus becomes more intense. This is because, as you get more familiar with the present moment, it will begin to occupy a larger portion of your attention. Eventually, you may find that you are able to meditate for long periods of time without getting bored or thinking about anything other than your breathing. In time, you may find that you can do this for just a few minutes at a time or for several hours during the day. Eventually, you will discover what works best for you and your schedule. There are many different ways to practice mindful breathing. The most common way is to sit in a quiet place and just notice the sensations in your body as you breathe in and out.

You can also practice mindful breathing while walking, working or doing any activity that requires concentration. Why Should You Practice Mindful Breathing? If you have ever taken a yoga class, you have probably noticed that some people have a much easier time concentrating on their breath than others. Some people find it very easy to focus on the present moment, while others find it difficult to stay focused on anything other than their thoughts. If you are a person who struggles with focusing your attention on one thing for an extended period of time, you may find that practicing mindful breathing is helpful. It is recommended that you start with 10 minutes of practice a day and gradually build up to 20 minutes or more each day. You may also find that you become less anxious or stressed after practicing mindfulness meditation. You may also notice that your ability to focus your attention improves and that your mind becomes more calm and peaceful. As a result, you may be able to deal with problems in a better way. When you practice mindful breathing, you are learning how to control your thoughts and emotions. This is an important skill for everyone, whether they suffer from anxiety or not. How to Practice Mindful Breathing There are many different ways to practice mindful breathing. Below are two easy techniques that you can use to begin practicing.

- Sit in a comfortable position and place your right hand on your chest. Notice the sensations of your breathing as you inhale and exhale. Allow your hand to be heavy so that you are aware of the movement of your breath. Focus on your breathing

51

and notice how it feels as you inhale and exhale. Your breathing should feel like a gentle flow of air through your nose, mouth, and lungs. If you notice that your mind is wandering off, gently bring it back to the present moment and focus on your breathing.

- Place your left hand on your stomach. Notice the sensations of your breathing as you inhale and exhale. Allow your hand to be light so that you are aware of the movement of your breath. Focus on your breathing and notice how it feels as you inhale and exhale. Your breathing should feel like a gentle flow of air through your nose, mouth, and lungs. If you notice that your mind is wandering off, gently bring it back to the present moment and focus on your breathing.

Practice Mindful Walking.

Walking is a good way to practice mindfulness. It is a simple activity that we all do daily. However, it's easy to get caught up in your own thoughts when you're walking. When you walk, be mindful of your surroundings, your body, and your thoughts. Walk slowly and focus on the ground beneath your feet. Pay attention to the temperature of the air and the sounds around you. You can also practice mindful breathing as you walk. Try to avoid rushing around. Take your time and enjoy the journey. Here are a few tips for practicing mindfulness while you walk:

- Be aware of your surroundings. Notice what you see when you look around.

- Be alert to any objects that catch your eye. Make note of what you notice.

- Be aware of your body. Try to pay attention to your body as you walk.

- Notice how you feel. Do your feet hurt? Do you experience any pains or aches? Do you feel tired? Do you have any stress or tension in your body?

- Pay attention to your thoughts. Walking can be a good way to clear your mind of all those distractions. Notice your thoughts and how they affect your mood. If you notice that you are having negative thoughts, it's okay to let them go. You don't have to judge yourself for being distracted. You can just let them go and continue walking. Try to think positive thoughts as you walk. Feel the joy of being alive. Breathe deeply. Focus on your breathing as you walk. You can start with slow, deep breaths in and out. Notice the air around you. Is it cold or warm? Is it damp or dry? How does it smell? Observe the scenery. You can focus on your surroundings as you walk. Do you notice any smells? What colors do you see? Do you notice anything that catches your eye? Take note of your senses. Pay attention to your senses. Notice what you hear and what you feel. Pay attention to the ground beneath your feet. Feel the ground with your feet and pay attention to what you feel. If you have been practicing mindfulness for a while, you may be able to do this easily. If you're new to mindfulness, you may find that walking meditation is a bit challenging at first. However, with practice, it will become easier and easier to stay mindful as you walk.

Make sure you have a clear and unobstructed path as you walk. Avoid walking in the street or on any side-walks. If there are people around, try to walk where they can't see you. This will make it much more difficult to get distracted. Choose a quiet area where there aren't many distractions. You can walk by yourself or with someone else. It's better if there is no one else around. If there are other people around, it will be more difficult for you to practice mindfulness. Find a place that is free of all distractions. You can find these places in parks, near bodies of water, or even in nature. Find a place that is easy to access. You don't have to travel far to get to this location. Just a short distance will do. Wear comfortable, loose-fitting clothes. Wear clothes that allow you to move comfortably. Avoid wearing shoes that have a hard sole. You should be able to feel the ground beneath your feet as you walk. Try to wear no jewelry. This includes watches, rings, and anything else that could potentially be a distraction. Try to keep your cell phone in your pocket. If you do happen to need to use your cell phone while you are walking, pull it out and use it with one hand. That way, you won't have to hold it in your pocket with the other hand, which may cause you to lose track of where you put it. Carry no bags or containers with you. This will help you avoid getting distracted by looking for stuff in your bag or carrying case. You can begin your practice by simply taking a few steps and paying attention to your senses as you walk. Try to focus on only one thing at a time. For example, if you are focusing on your breathing, don't think about anything else. Don't watch the scenery or try to notice anything else that is around you. Just breathe in and breathe out. Do this for five minutes. Then, see if you can increase the length of time that you meditate. If you want to, you can extend the time that you walk. Just make sure that you are still aware of your surroundings. You should pay attention to your body as you walk. Do you feel tired? If so, stop meditating and take a rest. When you meditate, it's not necessary to achieve a certain state. However, when you rest, it is important to get re-energized. After you meditate and rest, get back up on your feet and continue walking.

Exercise Mindful Listening

Listening is another activity that we do every day. But we often don't pay attention to what we hear. This is one of the easiest ways to become more mindful. It is a good idea to practice mindfulness meditation by listening. Just like with eating, you want to be aware of the sounds around you. Notice the smells, the light, and the temperature of the room.

This will help you ground yourself in the present moment. Also, when you are learning something new or something you have not learned for a long time, it is a good idea to pay close attention to what you are hearing. What you are about to learn may be the most important thing you will ever learn. Pay attention to every word and pay attention to how the speaker says the word. You should be especially attentive to anything that is not coming out of the speaker's mouth. This is called non-verbal communication.

While you are listening, think about what you are thinking and feeling. Do you feel nervous? Does your body feel tense? Are you listening with an open mind? Can you hear the words clearly? What did you hear? What is the meaning of the words? How does the speaker sound? What is his or her tone of voice? Is he or she angry? Happy? Happy and angry? Sad? Are you getting messages? If you are listening to someone speak, try to notice any sounds that are coming from the environment. How can you use these sounds to help you pay attention to what the speaker is saying? If you are having trouble hearing the speaker, put your hand over your ear and listen more closely. How can you change your physical position so that you can hear the speaker better? What can you do to help your listening skills? If you are being interviewed, how can you make it easier on yourself to pay attention to the questions being asked? Can you answer them in writing or on paper? Do you want to write down your answers and listen to them later? Or would you rather have the interviewer write down your answers? Can you look at your watch and say when you want to stop?

Remember, you are unique.

"There is no one else exactly like you in the world," says Dr. Alfred Hillary. You were born with a unique personality and a unique set of skills and talents. The way other people see you is only because of the way you choose to present yourself. Don't compare yourself to others. Instead, focus on how you can be the best version of yourself. "

People are different. No matter what anyone else thinks, you should be yourself. You should do what makes you happy. If you do that, you will feel better about yourself and become more confident. There's nothing wrong with being different. So don't be afraid to show the world who you really are. It's good to have a different personality than the people around you. Don't be afraid to stand out; just be confident in yourself. Be yourself.

I'm not sure I would say it is a bad thing for one to be different. For some people, that might mean a different skin tone, eye color, or height. For others, it might mean being part of a different religion, race, gender, or sexual orientation. It's good to be different. People are different. Everyone has their own quirks. If we were all exactly the same, life wouldn't be very interesting. If we were all the same, we wouldn't have any uniqueness. It's good to have different people around us. It's good to have different cultures, religions, and ways of thinking.

You should not get jealous of other people's lives or their success. Don't be too critical of other people or judge them. You will also never be happy when you are critical of others. Don't let your jealousy take over your mind and emotions. We all have things that we are not proud of, but it is how you deal with them that determines how you'll be in life.

Stop worrying about what other people think.

Instead, worry about how you can make other people think well of you. That is the true measure of your success in life. People will always have an opinion about you. Either good or bad, It is your choice whether you let them influence you. If they like you, great. If not, that's OK too. The point is, you don't have to convince everyone to like you. The point is to convince those who matter to you. Don't let anyone get to you. Keep your head up high, look them in the eye and speak from your heart. Be honest and truthful, and don't let anyone see you as vulnerable. Don't let anyone bring you down. Stay positive. Always look on the bright side of life. even if it is difficult. even when things are going badly. Look for the good in everything. It will always be there. Find it. Embrace it. Use it to power yourself up. Everything is a lesson. Even the bad. Even failure. Failure is simply an opportunity to learn something new. So what if someone else got the job you wanted? What if someone else got all the money they needed? What if someone else got the girl/boy they loved? Life is not about us. It's about everyone else. It's about them and how we can help them. It's only about us when we let it be. When we get lost in our own selfish thoughts, When we start thinking about ourselves and our own wants and needs, That is the biggest mistake we can make in life. Always think of others. Always put their needs before your own. What do you want to be when you grow up? I bet you already know the answer to that question. I bet you have a specific vision for your future. Maybe you want to be a doctor. A teacher An artist Maybe you want to own a business. Become a pilot. Or a rock star. The point is, whatever it is you want to do, you've already thought about it. You've got a picture in your mind's eye of what that life will look like. And now it's time to take that picture and make it come to life.

Practice gratitude.

The idea behind this is to be grateful for all the things that you have. When you are grateful, you will feel more positive about yourself and the people around you. You will be more motivated and you will find it easier to make decisions and solve problems. If you are not feeling positive about yourself or your life, then it is important that you try to find a way to make yourself feel better. When you do this, you will also make others around you feel better. When we are stressed out, we tend to worry about the future. We worry about things like, "What if I don't get my work done on time?" or "What if I fail the test?" As a result of worrying about the future, we end up stressed out. This can cause us to act in certain ways, such as yelling at our children or having arguments with our spouses. But we can learn to control our stress by taking time to reflect on the past and the future. We can do this by writing down our thoughts and feelings. We can also practice gratitude. The idea behind this is to be grateful for all the things that you have. When you are grateful, you will feel more positive about yourself and the people around you. You will be more motivated and you will find it easier to make decisions and solve problems. There are many benefits to mindfulness. One of them is that it can help us live a happier life. This is because we are able to control our emotions, which allows us to be in the present moment. Another benefit of mindfulness is that it helps us become more positive. It helps us see things from a different perspective. This is because when we are mindful, we are less focused on our thoughts and feelings. We are also able to see things as they really are, rather than how we think they are. We can also learn to become more flexible, which will allow us to deal with unexpected events.

When we practice mindfulness, we learn to accept things as they are. We learn to be "non-judgmental" about our thoughts and feelings. This does not mean that we do not have any thoughts or feelings. It simply means that we do not allow those thoughts or feelings to control us. For example, if you are feeling stressed out, it is important to recognize that you are feeling stressed out. But it is also important to not allow your feelings of stress to take over your life. When you do this, it will be much easier to find a solution to your problem. If you are having trouble focusing on your work, it is important to recognize that you are having trouble focusing on your work. But it is also important to not allow your feelings of being unfocused to take over your life. When you do this, it will be much easier to find a solution to your problem.

Gratitude helps us become more positive. It also gives us a sense of purpose. We can develop the skill of being mindful by doing things like counting our blessings or by writing down what we are grateful for. It is important to do these activities every day. Try to do them first thing in the morning and before you go to sleep. It is surprising how often we fail to be mindful during the day because we get caught up in our "swirl" of thoughts and feelings. The practice of gratitude will help bring you back to the present moment. It will also help you see the world from a different perspective. This will make it easier for you to deal with unexpected events. Count your blessings. Write down what you are grateful for. We can develop the skill of being mindful by doing things like counting our blessings or by writing down what we are grateful for. It will also help you see the world from a different perspective. This will make it easier for you to deal with unexpected events. Mindfulness is an important part of living a happier life.

Summary

Mindfulness is the practice of being aware of your present circumstances without judgment. You can learn to be more mindful by paying attention to the things you do daily. Being mindful is like exercising your brain; the more you do it, the easier it will get. Here are six ways to become more mindful. When you notice your thoughts, you will learn to stop and focus on the present.

This exercise will help you gain control over your thoughts. You can practice noticing your thoughts when you are reading, playing a game, or taking a walk. It will also help you stop thinking about the past or the future. When you are feeling upset, your mind is not thinking clearly. The more upset you get, the worse your thoughts become.

It is helpful to be aware of what you are thinking so that you can learn to control your thoughts. Practice noticing your emotions by doing something simple, such as eating. To practice mindfulness, you need to be aware of your thoughts, feelings, and emotions. You also need to train your brain to pay attention in the present moment. Most time, we are not aware of our emotions and feelings.

It is important to learn how to identify them. Mindful breathing is an ancient meditation practice that can help increase your overall sense of well-being. It takes practice, but it is very easy to learn. Eventually, you may find that you can meditate for long periods of time without getting bored or thinking about anything other than your breathing. Some people have an easier time concentrating on their breath than others.

When you practice mindful breathing, you are learning how to control your thoughts and emotions. It is recommended that you start with 10 minutes of practice a day and gradually build up to 20 minutes each day. Mindful walking is a good way to practice mindfulness. Pay attention to the sensations of your breath as you inhale and exhale. Walk slowly and focus on the ground beneath your feet.

Notice what you see when you look around you and pay attention to objects that catch your eye. Staying mindful while walking can help you clear your mind of all those distractions. Pay attention to your thoughts and how they affect your mood as you walk. If you're new to mindfulness, it may be a bit challenging at first, but it will get easier with practice. Make sure you have a clear and unobstructed path as you walk.

Choose a quiet area where there aren't many distractions. Avoid walking in the street or on any side-walks. If there are people around, try to walk where they can't see you.

CHAPTER 3

The Habit Of Thinking To Get Things Done

We all have a bad habit of thinking. This is something that has always been with us since the beginning of our lives. As children, we tend to be impulsive and don't think before we act. Our parents tried their best to teach us the right way to do things, but we were not willing to listen to them. As adults, we are still very much like children when it comes to this matter. There are so many people who get into trouble because of their inability to control themselves. It's also a problem for some people to pay their bills on time, make their appointments, and plan their finances. If you notice yourself doing these things often, there must be a reason behind them. One of the reasons why you are doing this is that you haven't learned how to manage your time and money effectively. It's not that you do not know how to manage your time and money; you just don't want to. The thing is that you want to live like everyone else. You want to have your own home, a car, and a job. As long as you can have all these things, you will be happy with your life. When you think about it, this is all because of our bad habit of thinking. We are still unable to stop ourselves from thinking about making things happen.

When we try to do something new, we have to work very hard to accomplish it. We should think ahead of time about how to get through with what needs to be done. This makes the job easier. For example, if you don't know how to cook, you can ask someone else. You will also save some money if you cook for yourself because you can buy everything in bulk. You need to plan your grocery list before you go shopping. This helps you to save money on food. You can even cook a complete meal.

This is a great way to save money. It is a good idea to write down what you need to do before you start working. This makes the work easier and less stressful. You can make this a habit and continue it throughout your life.

The idea here is that if you can get your mind in the right frame of mind and be a little more productive, you'll experience a noticeable uptick in your sense of well-being. And that, my friend, is true productivity. When you become productive and eliminate the mental clutter, your brain becomes clearer and, therefore, you begin to feel less stressed and more at peace.

I've found that this is easier said than done. I'm not sure if it's because we live in a society that tells us to always be "on" or if it's just because I'm naturally a little lazy. But, it's definitely true that the less time you spend worrying about the past and the future, the more time you'll have to focus on the present. If you're ready to take the plunge and try this for yourself, here are some tips on how to do it:

- **Make a list of all the things that are stressing you out.** You'll be surprised at how many of them you've pen down. If you're really having trouble, make a list of everything. And, then, put a check mark next to the ones that are really bugging you. Don't be afraid to go through all of them, especially if they're all important to you. It's only when we start to let go of the things that aren't that big a deal that we can truly be free from stress.

- **Get rid of the things that don't matter.** If you're going through your list and checking off the ones that really stress you out, and there are still a few things left that you feel are important, take those off too. By letting go of the things that don't really matter, you'll be surprised at how much less stressed you'll be. You'll also find yourself more productive.

- **Take time to do something you love.** This will help you to be happier in the present moment. If you can't find something that makes you happy, it's probably time to take stock of your life and make some changes. There's always something that you can do to make yourself feel better such as having a positive attitude. Even when things seem bad, there are always ways to improve things. For example, if you're having a rough day at work, instead of complaining about how awful your boss is or how unfair life is, think about what you can do to make yourself happier in the long run.

- **Don't try to do everything at once.** It's not realistic, and you'll end up feeling like a failure. Instead, start by doing one thing at a time. Then, after you complete that, try another. And so on. By starting with one small change and seeing how it makes you feel, you'll be able to build on that feeling and add more to your day.

- **Learn to say "no".** If there's something you need to do but it's not really important, then don't do it. If you have a friend that needs help, then give them the help they need. But, if you don't know if it's really important or not, then don't do it.

- **When you're feeling stressed, take a deep breath.** Count to four, and when you're ready, exhale. This will help you clear your head and relax.

- **Take time to get enough sleep.** Getting a good night's rest will make you feel more relaxed and help you be more productive.

- **When you have free time, find something that**

76

interests you. Reading a good book or listening to music can be a great way to relax and enjoy yourself.

- **When you're doing something that you don't like, try to think of it as a means to an end.** If you don't want to do something, then use it as motivation to do something you do want to do.

- **If you feel that you need to talk to someone, talk to them.** If you have a friend who's going through something similar, tell them how they're feeling.

- **If you're feeling sad, don't bottle it up.** Tell your friend or family member how you're feeling. They may be able to help you out.

- **Don't dwell on the past.** If you've done something in the past that you regret, learn from it and move on. Don't beat yourself up over it. It's gone. Move forward.

- **Don't look to the future.** When you get anxious, you begin to worry about things that haven't even happened yet.

- **Don't try to change other people.** If you're having problems with a friend or family member, just keep it to yourself and let them work things out for themselves.

- **Don't try to control everything that happens to you.** If something is going to happen, then let it happen. Life will take care of itself if we let it.

- **Let go of perfectionism.** There's no such thing. We all have our flaws. It's up to us to find the beauty in those flaws and to learn from them.

- **If you're feeling overwhelmed by your responsibilities, then delegate some.** If you can afford to hire someone to do something for you, then do so. Stop thinking about how to make it all work and start thinking about how to make the best of what you already have. You'll be amazed at how much lighter you'll feel.

Thinking to make things done will help you to get out of trouble and stay on top of your goals. This habit has made my life easier. I find that most people get in trouble when they don't do what they should do. They don't do their work, and this results in failure. They also don't get the things that they want. We have to be consistent when we are trying to achieve our goals. The more consistent we are, the better we are at achieving our goals. The more we achieve our goals, the better we feel about ourselves. I have always been consistent with my studies and I have never let my grades slip. If you can stay focused on your goal, then you can stay on top of it.

We can say that we are going to take time and energy to do something but the thing is that we don't actually do it. The first step to getting anything done is planning to get it done. You have to think about what you want and how you are going to do it. So, you should decide to do it before you actually do it. You have to make a plan so you can set the steps that you will follow and complete the plan. You have to be clear about what you want to accomplish. The best way to do this is to make a list. You can use the list to help you in the planning stage, and if you have already decided to do something, you can use the list to remind you of what you want to do. Your plans should be clear and easy to understand.

One of the best ways to get things done is to simply start doing them. Don't over-think things. Many people wait until they are "sure" that they should do something before they actually do it. This is a very slow way to get anything done. If you have a project to do and you are not sure how to do it, ask someone who has done a similar project before. Most likely, they will be more than happy to share their ideas with you. Don't wait for "certainty". Certainty never arrives. In life, we always have to deal with "uncertainty". Make no mistake about it:

- Most of life is uncertain!

- Don't waste time waiting for certainty!

- Just do it!

- Action is the antidote to indecision!

The Habits of Highly Successful People

There is a great secret about success and happiness. It's really simple. You have to think and act as if you're already successful and happy. The moment you realize that you are not doing well in anything, you should start acting as if you're a winner. That means, you should try to be confident and cheerful. If you feel depressed or down, you should always look for a way to overcome these feelings. It's possible to do this by looking at the bright side. Instead of thinking about the bad things, you should focus on the good things. You should keep on believing that everything will work out in your favor.

You must know how to plan your time so that you will have enough time to do all the things that you need to do. This is an important habit to be able to control your time. There is no way that you can be successful if you don't have good time management skills.

In fact, people who have good time management skills have better relationships with others than those who don't. It's also true that if you don't get your priorities straight, you will never achieve your goals. Your success is based on how much time you put into your work. It's really hard to be successful if you don't make a priority out of your time. If you spend your time working instead of having fun, you'll never be happy. You have to learn how to prioritize your tasks so that you won't run yourself ragged trying to do everything at once.

If you want to be more organized, the first thing that you need to do is to make sure that you have a schedule that you can keep track of. If you don't have one, you will never be able to stay on top of your priorities. You must also set aside some time each week for the things that you have to do. You need to put a priority on these things and do them even when you are busy with other tasks. You will need to find out what you can accomplish in a day. It is possible to get much more done in a day than you think. You need to decide how many hours per day you can work before you start getting burned out. To be successful, you need to figure out your priorities. You should set aside time for the important things and make sure that you do not overwork yourself.

Having good habits is another characteristics successful people posses. Some people think that they are too busy to practice good habits, but this is not true. You can start today to build good habits into your daily life. The most important thing to remember is to be consistent. You should do the same thing every day. You should always keep your promises and do what you say you will do. This is because people know what you say and they will believe you when you tell them that you will do a certain thing. Don't make empty promises, but keep your promises. The next thing you need to do is to be honest with yourself and other people. Don't lie to yourself or others. Be yourself, and be open to new ideas and experiences. You may be shocked to find out that you are not the only person who has been through the same situation. There are a lot of people who have had the same experience and you can learn from their mistakes.

One of the thing you should have at the back of your mind is that if you want to be a successful person, you have to develop the habits of successful people. Here are the five things successful people do every day that make them successful:

They always try to improve their skills and abilities.

They are always trying to learn new things. Why? Simply because they're driven by a powerful emotion called "ambition". Ambition is the engine that makes the train run. It is what gets you out of bed every morning. It is what keeps you going when the road gets tough. It is what propels you past the obstacles in your life. Ambition is what allows you to accomplish great things. It's not selfish, it's not greedy. It is simply a desire to do better than you did yesterday. It is a desire to improve your ability to perform at your best. Ambition is what drives you to become a better person.

They are always working hard at improving their performance.

No matter how successful they have been in the past, they won't rest on their laurels and think everything is perfect just because it is "business as usual". They are always on the lookout for new ways to make things better. To increase sales. To cut costs. To do it all with less effort. And they don't stop. In this day and age, when it's all about "the bottom line", the way a company operates has a direct impact on its future. If you want to make money, if you want to have a long term sustainable success, if you want to build a company that will be there in 10 years time, you must be ready to change. You must always be looking to improve.

They always do their best to succeed.

And they are very proud of that. They will work as long as necessary to accomplish their goal. As a business owner, you know this to be true. But when it comes to making the ultimate decision in their life, it's not about money or the success of the company. It's about what is best for their family and the impact that they want to make on others.

They keep their focus on achieving their goals and objectives.

They are results-oriented. They know that it is not enough to have a good idea. You must also have a good person to implement the idea. A good person is one who can take your idea, run with it and achieve spectacular results for you. This is a rare commodity and usually much more valuable than a good idea. They are hungry. This is the most important quality of all.

Hunger drives people to succeed. It is a terrible thing

when someone gets in their way and is "crowded out" by a more driven person. These people are not selfish or greedy. They simply don't see why they should wait around for others to give them a chance. When I was growing up, my father used to tell me that opportunity doesn't knock very hard at anyone who is busy pushing against the door. Opportunity waits for no man. This is especially true in an entrepreneurial venture. If you are not in motion, if you are not reaching for the brass ring, then... Opportunity Won't Come To You! And you will miss out on the fun, the thrill, and the amazing sense of achievement that comes with grabbing hold of it when it comes knocking at your door.

They never give up.

You can use these habits to be more successful. Always strive to get better at what you do. You can't accomplish anything if you don't keep trying. It is important to try your best and never quit. Don't let anyone tell you that you can't achieve your goals. You should be motivated to do what you can do to improve your success. Your success depends on what you do, not on what other people do. If you have a goal in mind, it is best to focus your energy on achieving that goal. That's the way to be successful.

13 Habits That Will Make You More Productive (and Less Miserable)

I know you're probably thinking that being productive is difficult because it takes a lot of time and energy. There is a lot more to it than just getting up and going to work, right? Yes. But, if you want to make sure that you have a productive day, then there are some things that you need to do. Some of these things are things that you should do every day, but others you need to do only once or twice a week. The next thing that you should do is to be focused. It's good to take a break every now and then, but make sure that you don't procrastinate. There's nothing worse than starting a task and then losing focus after two minutes. You should also keep your goals in mind. If you don't have goals, you won't be productive. The next thing that you need to do is be prepared. This means that you need to know where you

want to go and what you're going to do when you get there. When you're not prepared, you'll find that you're always running behind. So, it's best to be prepared, even if you have some time to spare. The next thing that you need to do is to be organized. You'll find that being organized will help you stay on track and make sure that you're not wasting time. If you are organized, then you'll also be able to focus better. It's not always easy to do everything yourself, but you can ask for help if you feel overwhelmed or if you're having trouble doing something.

Having help can make a big difference in your productivity. You should take a break every once in a while. This doesn't mean that you have to stop working. You just need to take a break from what you're doing. If you do this every day, you'll notice that you'll start to get more productive. Get more things done in less time with this productivity measures:

Create a daily ritual.

It may seem like a daunting task, but the most successful people do it, and it doesn't take much time at all. I'd recommend taking a few minutes every day to get into a routine. For example, if you are trying to start your day with a new habit, I would recommend waking up 15 minutes early and doing your morning ritual. This will give you time to prepare yourself for the day. Start small.

Don't try to do too much all at once. Just one little thing will be a huge accomplishment. Start with the things you know you should do. I'm not kidding when I say this is an important element of success. Most people think that in order to be successful, they have to do everything first-class. They have to dress impeccably, eat well, exercise, have a perfect personal and professional life.

It's a good start, but the real secret is to start with the things you know you should do. The rest will follow. Stop doing what you hate. This may seem like a simple step, but it's not. You must stop doing things that you hate. If you do something you dislike, then you'll always be unhappy. You can't always be happy if you are doing something that makes you miserable. You have to take the time to identify what you don't like about your job, your relationships, your finances, or your health. Once you've identified the areas that make you unhappy, it's time to eliminate them from your life. When I was a teenager, my parents told me that I would never amount to anything because I didn't want to play football. I had no interest in sports. I was more interested in been an event planner. However, my parents were firm in their belief that I needed to play football in order to become a success.

It took me over 20 years to get to where I am today. It's easy to get caught up in the day-to-day details of life. You may think that if you just work harder, you'll be successful. You may think that if you just get a better job, you'll be happy. If you are working for someone else, they will make you miserable if you don't do exactly what they want you to do. If you are not in control of your life, then you will always feel unfulfilled. I've seen people make hundreds of thousands of dollars and still not be happy. It's not how much money you make, it's how much money you make compared to your goals and desires. It's important to remember that you have complete control over your life. You are responsible for your own happiness and success. This is the most important lesson that I have learned. Take time to reflect on your successes. I'm sure you've heard this advice before, but it's worth repeating. People who are successful are always reflecting on their successes. They don't take things for granted. They are always looking at what they have accomplished and what they can do next. They don't dwell on what they don't have. Instead, they focus on what they do have. I'm a big fan of reflection. It's a great way to get to know yourself. You can learn a lot from your successes. If you're not careful, you may become too focused on your failures. It's easy to get stuck in the past and look at your failures. However, if you want to be successful, you need to focus on your successes. Ask yourself what you want. Successful people have goals. If you are struggling, you should ask yourself why. What do you want? What are your goals? If you aren't clear about your goals, then you won't know when you have achieved them. When you know what you want, you will know whether or not you are making progress. When you know what you want, it's much easier to achieve it. Be willing to make sacrifices. If you want to be successful, you must be willing to make sacrifices.

Set realistic goals.

If you are a beginner, you should start with small steps and make them more and more difficult as you progress. You can also take help from your friends and relatives to help you in achieving your goals. They can motivate you and support you through the process. It is always better to work alone than with someone else. This way you will be able to learn what to do and what not to do.

It's always a good idea to set realistic goals. This is one of the most important things to remember when you are trying to achieve a goal. Don't set unrealistic goals. Be more realistic. Also, it is better to set short-term goals than long-term goals. Don't set too many goals at once because you will have trouble reaching them all. If you set a goal for the future and don't try to reach it, it will be very difficult for you to achieve that goal. Always make sure that you are able to reach the goal.

We should set goals to accomplish our desired results. This will help us achieve our dreams. Setting goals is a great way to motivate yourself. It helps you stay focused on your desires. When we have a goal in mind, it's easier for us to do things that we want to do. Our mind is focused on a certain direction. If we don't have any goals, we will never accomplish anything in life. Achieving our goals will be easy if we set realistic goals. It is important to be realistic in your efforts because you may feel disappointed if your goal is not attained. You should not set a high expectation for yourself. This will cause you to be frustrated and give up.

For example, if you ask someone to hold you back just because you are afraid of failure, then it is very likely you will fail. On the other hand, if you do it all by yourself, then you will learn very quickly what to do and what not to do. So, find out what you really want to achieve and go for it! Don't worry about failing. Just keep trying and don't give up. The only people who never make mistakes are those who never try.

Find meaning in your work.

Work is a very important part of our lives. We have to do it to earn a living and to have a future. We need to work hard to get a good job and to get ahead. People often tell us to find meaning in our work. If we don't, we will be miserable and depressed. It can be difficult to find the meaning in our work, especially when we are doing the same thing over and over again. This is why I am glad that I found a way to find the meaning in my work. I find my work meaningful when I help people. By helping others, I can make their lives better and make them happier. What they tell me about my work, it helps me to feel good about myself.

When you work on something that you don't enjoy, you won't be able to complete it. This is true of anything. In order to be able to get something done, you must have a positive attitude. When you do this, you will be motivated to do whatever you need to do to get the task completed. Your attitude plays a role in getting things done. You can choose to be positive or negative. The choice is yours.

It is important to find the meaning in your work. People who are happy at their jobs have found their place in life. This makes them feel important. They are proud of their achievements. People who have a passion for their work feel important. It gives them a sense of achievement and fulfillment.

Take time off.

To make yourself feel better, you should try to take some time off. This will help you to relax and have a good time. You should also take some time to do things that you enjoy. This will help you to feel more relaxed and happier. However, you should not let too much time pass because it may lead you to do some things you shouldn't be doing. You should not let yourself get bored with doing the same old things all the time. You should find something new to do that is different from what you usually do. Doing the same thing every day is boring. If you are doing the same thing all the time, it's almost like a habit. Habits are good, but you should try to break the habits when you are getting bored. If you feel tired, you should take time off. You should rest and avoid the hard physical work. There are lots of things that we can do to help us relax. You can get a massage or have a pedicure. You can also read a book or watch a movie. You should try to do things that are fun and interesting. This will make you feel more active and energetic.

Find a mentor.

Finding a mentor is important because it is the best way to reach your goals.. Ask a friend, a family member, a colleague, or a teacher who has achieved success in their life for help. Your mentor will be able to guide you on the way to success and also help you to grow as a person. A mentor can provide guidance to you. A good mentor will listen to you. Your mentor can help you to develop your potential and give you advice.

You may not realize this, but most people need guidance and support when they are young. A mentor is someone who has been through life and knows the hard work and the difficulties that it can entail. Mentors have more life experience than you do. They can help you avoid making mistakes and they can guide you as you grow up and become successful. As you grow older, you will probably meet a lot of new mentors. People who are successful are usually successful because they surround themselves with people who have done great things and they learn from them. That's why it's important to be around people who can help you to be a better person.

Have a support system.

Everyone needs a support system. This is especially true for people who are trying to accomplish something big in their lives. Don't be afraid to reach out for help. Don't be too proud to accept help either. It is important to have people in your life who will encourage you and give you good advice. Real friends and family will do that, but also consider other people who can help you. It's good to have friends, but it's even better to have a strong support system. This is a group of people who will be there for you when you need them. They'll help you through the tough times and celebrate with you when you accomplish something great. This is a critical key to success. Don't work alone. Work in a group. Find out what kind of group works best for you. Some people like to work in groups with other people who have the same goals as they do. Other people enjoy working in groups with people who have opposing goals. One thing is certain: you will never get anywhere by yourself. The first step to creating a strong support system is to create one or more "support groups". A support group is simply a small group of people (two or three) who are committed to helping each other. Look in the phone book under "People To List" or "Personals". Look under "Coaches", "Consultants", "Teachers", "Mentors", and any other heading that describes a person who might be willing to help you. Consider any help you get from these sources.

If nothing else, just talking with someone who has been where you are will be of benefit to you. Consider everyone who offers to help as an ally in your quest for greatness.

Build a practice.

As I mentioned earlier, people will be more likely to listen to someone who knows how to talk to them. They will also listen more when someone is enthusiastic about the subject. Therefore, it's important that you build a practice of speaking with people. That way, you'll be able to improve your skills and become a great speaker. The first thing that you should do is to find out what is it you want to talk about. That is the most important thing to do if you want to improve. It's also important to make sure that the people that you are going to talk to understand your purpose. If you are going to speak at a company get together or event, then you should know what your speech is all about. Make sure that your listeners will be able to follow you. If they can't, then you won't be able to communicate properly.

A practice is an area of expertise you can build your own. You will have a practice once you figure out what you are good at. You will know if you are a good doctor because you won't be practicing medicine in the streets. You won't be a good lawyer if you don't practice law. A practice is something you can build yourself. It is something you can learn to do. It is something that you can do alone. The best way to build a practice is to start with something you are interested in and keep working on it until you are good at it. Then, you can start doing it for a living. If you work hard, you can make a lot of money.

Manage your time.

You should manage your time because you can't get

more of it. When you spend time with family and friends, do it wisely. If you are trying to be successful in life, you have to spend time working on your career and business. Spend time on what's important. If you don't manage your time, you won't be able to be successful. Don't worry about how much time you spend doing something. Just do it the best way possible. Try to work hard to be the best. Don't let anyone tell you that you are not good enough. You are worthy of being the best because you can achieve great things. You should always be motivated and positive about yourself. Have you ever wondered how people who work long hours manage to have such great time? The secret is that they plan their time carefully and they work hard to ensure that they don't waste their time. It's true that there is nothing worse than being a slacker. However, you don't need to be a workaholic either. People who are workaholics tend to be extremely stressed out. They often end up losing all of their free time. They become so busy working that they can't even enjoy themselves when they are off work. If you want to have a good balance between your work and leisure time, you need to spend time planning what you want to do each day. You can also get help from your friends to help you plan your time.

Keep yourself fit and healthy.

Being fit and healthy is important. It helps you to get along with other people. You'll feel better and you'll have more energy too. As a matter of fact, being fit and healthy makes you more attractive to people. It is important to do exercises regularly. You should also be conscious about what you eat. You should try not to eat too much and not too little. Avoid fast foods and junk foods as much as possible. Try to eat more fresh fruits, vegetables, and proteins. You'll have more energy if you do. If you want to lose weight, then do exercises and eat healthy. Exercise is the best way to lose weight. Don't forget to drink lots of water. Drink at least eight glasses of water every day. If you drink enough water, your body will feel better and you'll have more energy.

The next thing to do is to find a place to get into shape. You can visit a gym, join a gym, or take part in a program on television or the Internet. Whatever option you choose, make sure that you do it correctly. If you go to a gym, don't just sit and watch. You have to be active to get results. If you join a gym, try to find one that has a good staff. A good staff will motivate you to keep up with your workout routine. You can also get fit by taking part in a fitness program. There are many programs on television or the Internet. You can also go for a run or go swimming to get into shape. All these things are good ways to keep your body healthy and strong. If you are going to do something, make sure that you follow the directions that the program gives you. There is no doubt that we should try to be fit and healthy. This is because being fit and healthy will help you to have a good life. Also, you will be more successful at work and your relationships will be better with your friends and family.

Create a plan for work and life.

Take about five or ten minutes and create a plan for work and life. What I mean by this is write down everything you have to do today and every day for the next 30 days. Don't think about it too much; just do it. Start with the smaller things first such as writing an email or making a phone call. Once you get going, the list will get longer and longer. It's good to have goals but don't let yourself get overwhelmed. Just take one thing at a time and keep moving. As you accomplish one thing, move on to the next. If you run out of things to do, just keep repeating the same thing over and over. Don't be a perfectionist. Just keep moving and the things you do will get done.

Don't think about it too much; just do it!

Learn to say no.

Say no to people who make you feel uncomfortable, no to things that are not important, and no to things that don't help you achieve your goals. As a matter of fact, you should try to say "no" to everything. No means "no". You should always have a goal, and you must set a time to achieve it. Saying "yes" is a good thing, but saying "no" is also a good thing. Try to be honest and fair with yourself. Your success depends on the decisions you make. Make sure that the decisions you make are for the best. Don't let others decide for you. They may tell you that you can't because they are older, or you aren't smart enough, or you haven't done this or that. Don't let anyone get to you. If you think about it, there is no one better than you to do the things that you want to do. It is up to you to be the master of your destiny. Remember, you can't depend on someone else to help you; it's all up to you. You must help yourself. If you don't take care of yourself, nobody else will. The world is your oyster. It is your responsibility to keep your body in shape and

Seek out opportunities to learn new skills.

Everyone needs to keep up with the changing world, and one way to learn about this is to be open to different ways of doing things. If you don't like how things are done now, try to find a way to change it. Try to learn new skills and techniques, and you may be surprised at how much you can accomplish.

One of the best ways to be successful is to learn new things. When you start taking advantage of these opportunities, you will be on the right track. Make sure that you study and listen carefully whenever you have a chance to learn new things.

You must be creative in learning new things. Try taking courses and workshops that will help you to improve your ability to do things on a regular basis. One of the major step to find new skills is to have an open mind. You should be willing to try out different things. If you don't do that, you'll always be the same and not be able to improve your life. People who are very creative think out of the box and are able to do many things. You will never be successful without trying to learn new skills.

Take breaks and have fun.

You don't have to work all day, everyday. It is okay to take breaks and enjoy yourself. Go home early if you want to, or go out with friends to have a good time. It is a great way to unwind after a hard day of work. This is the only time that you can relax and let your hair down. You will enjoy yourself more when you take a break. There's no need to put on a happy face every single moment of the day. If you do this, you will become stressed and you won't be able to achieve anything at all. It's okay to take a break if you really need one. This is why you should have breaks in between your work. It is important to have fun and enjoy your life. Make sure to live life to its fullest every single day. It doesn't matter how hard or stressful the day is. You should have fun every single day of your life. Don't think about things that happen in the past or worry about things that might happen in the future. You need to concentrate on the present and enjoy it.

Summary

As children, we tend to be impulsive and don't think before we act. As adults, we are still unable to stop ourselves from thinking about making things happen. It is a good idea to write down what you need to do before you start working. When you become productive and eliminate the mental clutter, your brain becomes clearer and, therefore, you begin to feel less stressed and more at peace. By letting go of the things that don't really matter, you'll be surprised at how much less stressed you will be.

If you're having a bad day at work, think about what you can do to make yourself happier. Reading a good book or listening to music can be a great way to relax. If you need to talk to someone, talk to them. They may be able to help you. If you're feeling overwhelmed by your responsibilities, then delegate some of them.

If you can afford to hire someone to do something for you, then do so. Don't try to control everything that happens to you. Life will take care of itself if we let it. The first step to getting anything done is planning to get it done. Many people wait until they are "sure" that they should do something before they actually do it.

Don't wait for "certainty". Certainty never arrives. Action is the antidote to indecision! You must know how to plan your time so that you will have enough time to do all the things that you need to do. There is no way that you can be successful if you don't have good time management skills.

Your success is based on how much time you put into your work. Having good habits is another characteristic that successful people possess. You can start today to build good habits into your daily life. Here are the five things successful people do every day that make them successful: They always try to improve their skills and abilities.

They are driven by a powerful emotion called "ambition". They are always on the lookout for new ways to make things better. In this day and age, the way a company operates has a direct impact on its future. They know that it is not enough to have a good idea; you need a good person to implement it. Hunger drives people to succeed.

Always strive to get better at what you do. Don't let anyone tell you that you can't achieve your goals.

Being productive is more than just getting up and going to work every day. There are some things that you need to do in order to be more productive. In order to be successful, you must stop doing things that make you unhappy. Start with the things you know you should do and the rest will follow. Don't try to do too much all at once-just one little thing will be a huge accomplishment.

It's easy to get caught up in the day-to-day details of life. Take time to reflect on your successes. You are responsible for your own happiness and success. If you aren't clear about your goals, then you won't know when you have achieved them. If you are a beginner, you should start with small steps and make them more difficult as you progress.

Don't set too many goals at once because you will have

trouble reaching them all. Achieving our goals will be easy if we set realistic goals. I find my work meaningful when I help people and make their lives better. If you work on something that you don't enjoy, you won't be able to complete it. People who are happy at their jobs have found their place in life and are proud of their achievements.

To make yourself feel better, you should try to take some time off. This will help you relax and have a good time. If you are doing the same thing all the time, it's almost like a habit. Find a mentor to help you achieve your goals. Most people need guidance and support when they are young.

A mentor is someone who has been through life and knows the hard work and difficulties that it can entail. Mentors have more life experience than you do and can help you avoid making mistakes. Don't be afraid to reach out for help. Don't work alone. Find out what kind of group works best for you.

Some people like to work in groups with other people who have the same goals as they do. Others enjoy working in groups, even if they have opposing goals. Consider everyone who offers to help as an ally in your quest for greatness. People are more likely to listen to someone who knows how to talk to them. Therefore, it's important that you build a practice of speaking with people.

A practice is an area of expertise in which you can build your own. If you work hard, you can make a lot of money. If you are trying to be successful in life, you have to spend time working on your career and business. People who are workaholics tend to be extremely stressed out and lose all their free time. You don't need to be a workaholic either.

Being fit and healthy makes you more attractive to people. Exercise is the best way to lose weight. As much as possible, avoid fast foods and junk foods. Take part in a fitness program or go for a run or swim to get into shape. Don't forget to drink lots of water.

It's good to have goals, but don't let yourself get overwhelmed. Write down everything you have to do today and every day for the next 30 days. As you accomplish one thing, move on to the next. Don't be a perfectionist; just keep moving and things will get done. One of the best ways to be successful is to learn new things.

If you don't like how things are done now, try to find a way to change them. Take courses and workshops that will help you improve your ability to do things on a regular basis. You don't have to work all day, every day. It is okay to take breaks and enjoy yourself. There's no need to put on a happy face every single moment of the day. Go home early if you want, or go out with friends to have a good time.

CHAPTER 4

How To Make The Most Of Your Mind

The best thing you can do for yourself is to develop your mind. It's the most important part of you that will help you achieve your goals and achieve them well. There are many people who don't realize how much they're limiting themselves by not making the most of their minds.

You'll never get anywhere without using your mind to its full potential. That means developing your brain. We all have a brain, and it's the most important organ in our bodies. It's what we use to think with, and if we don't use it properly, it can cause a lot of problems.

Our brains are the most important part of our body. It is the most complex piece of machinery in the world. It is an amazing thing. It works so fast and it is able to remember so much. However, most of the time, we don't use nearly all of the power of our brains. We are so busy doing other things that we forget about the importance of our brains. Our brains are like a car engine. If we do not give it fuel, it will eventually stop working. This means that we need to use our brains every day. We need to let them rest and recuperate from the daily demands that we put on them. However, we also need to keep them at peak performance level so they can continue to help us throughout our entire life. The way to do this is to learn something new every day. It is the only thing that will keep our brains healthy and running at maximum efficiency. The way to learn something new is to read an interesting book, go for lectures, take an online class, go to a seminar or just talk with someone who has more knowledge than you. The way we let our brains recover is by doing nothing. By not thinking about anything for a period of time. Our brains need time to rest and recuperate.

It's no wonder that so many people don't know how to use their brains. They're not doing anything with it at all. This is why I want to share some of the most common ways to make the most of your mind. You'll see that you can do many things to make sure that you're using your brain to its full capacity. Develop Your Memory The first thing you should do to make the most of your mind is to develop your memory. This is something that everyone needs to be able to do. When you can remember something, you're more likely to be able to do something with it.

If you can't remember where you put your car keys, for example, you're going to have a hard time finding them and getting in your car and driving to work or wherever else you need to go. If you don't know something, it's hard for you to even start trying to learn it. It's like trying to walk across the room without taking a step. You just won't be able to do it. Most people are surprised at how much their memory works on automatic pilot. You don't have to think about what you want to remember. You simply have to remember it. The first step to doing this is to create a filing system for all of your important papers and documents. Keep them in a central place so you will be able to find them quickly. This is especially important if you are going to use your PC as your primary tool for working and studying. Make a list of your objectives.Write down on paper all of the goals you would like to achieve. Be sure to write them in the present tense. If you do this, it will help you stay focused on what you need to do now, instead of thinking about what you need to do in the future. If you wait until later to write down your goals, you're likely to forget them. By writing them down immediately, you'll be more likely to achieve them.

You can make a list of your goals or you can just write a short paragraph describing each one of them. If you want to improve your memory, you should also consider learning how to learn. How To Learn is One of the most common ways people try to learn is to study. The problem with this approach is that you only use 10% of your brain while you're studying. This means that you're not using any of your other 90% of your brain to help you learn. This is why many people end up being very frustrated when they try to learn something and can't seem to remember it later on. Learning can also be done by listening to audio tapes, watching videos, or reading books. Unfortunately, these methods don't involve the use of your brain in the process. Instead, they just use your eyes and ears. If you want to use all of your brain to learn, you have to use it during the learning process. This means that you need to do things like memorize a poem, study a foreign language, or even play a video game. Learn How To Learn, Use Your Brain For Math If you want to really make the most of your mind, you should try to make sure that your brain is being used for something. The reason why people don't make the most of their minds is because they don't know how to use them properly. If you want to learn math, you should think about how your brain works. There are three main parts of your brain: The cerebrum, The cerebellum, The medulla oblongata. The cerebrum is where your thoughts, memories, and emotions are located. It's also where your thinking and reasoning take place. You can think of the cerebrum as your "thinking brain". The cerebellum is where you have your emotions and feelings. It also controls your balance and coordination. The medulla oblongata is where your body is controlled by your brain. Your brain is a very powerful tool. It can be used for many things. One of these things is math. If you want to use your brain to do math, you need to use it for this purpose.

One of the best ways to make yourself more productive is to develop good study habits. Developing good study habits doesn't mean that you have to study for long hours every day. It does mean that you should start by setting aside a certain amount of time each day to study. This can be for 20 minutes or less each day. The first thing you should do when you start studying is to get rid of all the junk in your mind. You do this by emptying your mind. You do this by taking some time each day to relax and unwind. You do this by going for a walk, having some exercise, or doing some other type of physical activity. After you have emptied your mind, you should focus on one single subject for a period of time.

Remember these words: "FOCUS!" Focus means that you are totally concentrating on one subject for a period of time. It does not mean that you are ignoring everything else that is going on around you. If you are trying to study for an upcoming test or presentation, you should develop the ability to ignore the things that are going on around you. You do this by developing good study habits.

You should use your mind every day for the rest of your life. If you don't use your mind, the rest of your body will slowly start to shut down. Use your mind to think creatively. Use your mind to plan your work and your workouts. Use your mind to make your work more efficient. If you do this, your body will automatically become more energized, and you'll have a much more youthful appearance. In fact, you should try to use at least eight of your ten brain cells almost every day. Don't let anyone tell you that you don't have enough time to use your mind. You need to use your mind every day for the rest of your life. Never underestimate the power of using your mind. It's one of the best tools you have for success.

Talk to Your Body Like You Would to a Friend (or Your Pet) Your body is a living thing, just like your pet. It needs to be treated as such. You can treat your pet like you would any friend or loved one: with respect, kindness, and understanding. If you don't treat your body the same way, it will never be healthy. If you're a vegetarian, your body needs to eat meat, fish, and other animal products. If you're an athlete, your body needs carbohydrates and protein to help it recover from hard workouts. If you're a smoker, your body needs to breathe fresh air. If you're an alcoholic, your body needs to drink alcohol in moderation. If you're a drug addict, your body needs to be free of drugs. The more you treat your body well, the better it will be.

You can't expect your body to work the way you want if you don't treat it well. Think Positively Every Day, Think about what you'd like to accomplish that day. Think about how you can use your mind to make your life better. Don't think about the problems that you have; think about the solutions that you can come up with to overcome them. If you feel like you have a bad attitude or are in a bad mood, try to change your mindset and think positive thoughts. Instead of thinking negatively, think about the good things in your life. Think about all of the people who love you and care about you. Think about the things that you're grateful for. Think about the things that you can do to make your life better. Think about the things that you're going to accomplish. This will help you to be more positive and motivated every day. If you don't think positively, you'll never achieve anything. Don't Let Negative People Get to You Don't let negative people get to you. If someone is being mean to you, just think about how much better it would be if they weren't mean to you at all. If you really hate something or someone, it's only natural that you'd want to express yourself. However, if you're not careful, you can easily let this hatred affect you. If you find yourself getting upset or angry when someone is being mean to you, try to control your emotions. Don't let anyone tell you that you should take their negative energy and turn it into positive energy. Don't let anyone tell you that you should give up your beliefs and convictions. You need to believe in yourself, even when the world tells you that you can't do it. Stop being a victim! There are so many things in life that you have no control over. You can't control what other people do or say. You can't control whether or not you get sick. Never underestimate the power of using your mind. It's one of the best tools you have for success.

How to Use Your Mind for Success

It is possible to change your mind and your behavior for

success. The more you practice the habit of being positive, the more likely you are to become successful. The easiest way to be positive is to surround yourself with positive people. These people will influence you in a positive way. You also need to be careful about negative people. If you find yourself attracted to negative people, you should try to distance yourself from them. If you are not careful, you can be influenced by negative people and lose your sense of hope and confidence. Don't get into arguments with these people. Let go of all of your anger and frustration when dealing with them. Make a conscious effort to surround yourself with positive people who will support you.

Another way is to use your mind to think about how to reach your goals. You should also be focused and determined to accomplish your goals. This will help you to get your mind prepared for your next challenge. When you are motivated and excited to do something, your mind will be able to work better for you. To keep your mind focused on a goal, you need to think about it often.

Have you ever wondered why some people seem to be more successful than others? How do they manage to accomplish so much and achieve their goals? There are a lot of things that can affect our lives and the way we live it, but one thing that is constant is that we all have a mind. And if we don't use our mind, we will never get anywhere in life.

So what I am going to tell you here today is how to use your mind to make yourself as successful as possible. Many people think that being smart is the same as being successful. This is not true. Being smart is important, but it is only half of the equation. The other half is using your smartness in such a way that leads you to achieving your goals. Here are seven ways to use your mind to make yourself more successful:

Visualize yourself as the owner of the goal.

When you visualize, you're putting yourself in the situation, experiencing it from a first person perspective. The more you do this, the more you will start to feel the emotion and experience it with your whole body. When you visualize your goal, imagine it in detail. Imagine the feeling of accomplishment you'll have once you achieve it. What is it like to have a goal that you've already achieved? What does it look like to you? How does it feel? If you are having trouble visualizing, use a picture of what your goal looks like, or what you think it will feel like. Know that you are going to make mistakes along the way. Mistakes happen. We all make them. That's life. Mistakes are part of the process of achieving our goals. As long as you keep moving forward, they won't stop you from reaching your goal. Remember to forgive yourself for your mistakes.

Anticipate every detail of the process.

The details are very important to be successful, for example, do you need to prepare a presentation? What will you wear? Do you need to make a list of what you want to achieve? If you want to win in a competition, you should always check what your competitors are doing, what they are preparing and what they will say.

You have to know everything about your goal and you have to think that it is going to happen before you start working on it. It is important to know how the process will work and when you will achieve your goal. When you write down your goal, you should also think about how to implement it. For example, if you want to study in a university, you should choose your subject and your courses and then you should choose a good school and a good place where you can study.

Put yourself in the "zone".

It's hard to find an expert who doesn't agree that you can get better results by putting more focus into your practice. When you enter the zone, you are at the top of your game. You are relaxed, calm, and focused on what you are doing. You are performing at a high level. If you are thinking about other things, you will be less effective.

This is one of my favorite mantras, and I find it really useful. For me, it means focusing on the task at hand and thinking about nothing else. In some senses, it's the opposite of multitasking. When I say "think about nothing else," that doesn't mean "don't think about anything else." It just means thinking about the task at hand.

Set goals with specificity.

"I want to lose 20 pounds by the end of the year" is not specific. But "I want to lose the weight I gained from eating those don't-ask-questions cookies" is very specific.

Be specific!

Specificity will help you achieve your goal faster and with less hassle. Consider this example: Let's say you decide to run a 10K race. You could say you want to run that race in under an hour. Or you could say you want to run a half marathon. Both are very general goals, but the second one is more specific. It's much easier to work toward a specific goal than a general one. You can do the same thing with weight loss. If you want to lose 20 pounds, it's much easier to lose 10 pounds than it is to lose 20 pounds. It's easier to lose 20 pounds by the end of the year than it is to lose 20 pounds in a week.

Break down the goal into smaller parts.

Learn to always breakdown your goal into little parts. Let's say your goal is to lose weight. Well, you should probably start by breaking that down even further. Maybe your first part of the goal is to simply eat less. OK, now your second part of the goal is to cut out sweets. And, your third part of the goal is to cut back on the amount of fat that you eat.

Keep breaking down your goal into parts until you have so many parts that you can easily see how each part will help you to accomplish your overall goal. Then, go ahead and take one part of your goal at a time and work on it until you have completed it. Don't worry about the other parts of your goal. Just concentrate on completing the part that you are working on. Once you have accomplished that part, go on to the next part. This process will keep your energy level up and give you an "end result" focus.

Don't get confused by all this. Keep breaking down your goal into smaller and smaller parts until you can easily see how each part will help you to accomplish your goal. Then go ahead and take one part of your goal at a time and work on it until you have completed it. Don't worry about the other parts of your goal. Just concentrate

For example, if the goal is to "write a best-selling novel," then the first step would be to write a "preliminary" outline of the book. This outline should include only the major points you think the book will make (e.g., your thesis statement, the three main points you plan to make in your body copy, and so on).

Do not think about the goal.

Think about the process instead of the end result. Many people get caught up in the "end result" of a project and never become focused on the process. Don't worry about getting it right. Just keep going and don't get stuck on any particular part of the project. The important thing is to keep moving forward. If you do that, everything will work out fine. In the meantime, don't think about the goal. Think about each step you are taking as you are progressing towards the goal. That way, you won't get discouraged when you face obstacles. You'll be able to overcome these obstacles because you are not thinking about how to accomplish the goal. If you do think about the goal, you won't be able to move past the first obstacle. You'll think about what you have to do to accomplish the goal, and that will surely stop you. Think about the process instead. The goal will work itself out as you are working on the process.

Think positive!

There are many things that can make you feel good. You can read a book, go for a walk in the park, take a shower or simply watch a nice movie. But it's not only about what we do but also about how we feel while doing it. This is why you should try to create a positive mind set. You have to accept yourself as you are and stop focusing on what you don't have.

Always keep your mind and spirit optimistic. If you don't have good thoughts, you will end up with bad things. Always think of the best possible outcome, and this can help you to achieve your goals. It is important to be positive. You don't want to be negative. It's not good for you. Try to avoid negativity and pessimism. Your attitude is a big part of your success. It can change your life and the way you see things. It can even affect your health. If you are always thinking negatively, it can make you feel low.

Summary

The best thing you can do for yourself is to develop your mind. It's the most important part of you that will help you achieve your goals. Our brains are like car engines; if we don't give them fuel, they will eventually stop working. Most people are surprised at how much their memory works on automatic pilot. If you can't remember where you put your car keys, for example, you're going to have a hard time finding them.

Developing a good memory is something that everyone needs to be able to do. If you want to improve your memory, you should consider learning how to learn. There are three main parts of your brain: the cerebrum, cerebellum, and medulla oblongata. These are the areas where thoughts, memories, and emotions take place. Developing good study habits doesn't mean that you have to study for long hours every day.

You should start by setting aside a certain amount of time each day for studying. "Focus means that you are totally concentrating on one single subject for a period of time. If you're a vegetarian, your body needs to eat meat, fish, and other animal products. The more you treat your body well, the better it will be. Think positively every day. Think about how you can use your mind to make your life better.

If you don't think positively, you'll never achieve anything. Don't let negative people get to you. If someone is being mean to you, just think about how much better it would be if they weren't mean at all. This will help you be more positive and motivated every day. The more you practice being positive, the more likely you are to be successful.

To keep your mind focused on a goal, you need to think about it often. Being smart is only half of the equation. Use your intelligence in a way that leads you to achieving your goals. When you visualize, you're putting yourself in the situation from a first-person perspective. The more you do this, the more you will start to feel the emotion and experience it with your whole body.

You know that you are going to make mistakes along the way? It's much easier to work toward a specific goal than a general one. Specificity will help you achieve your goal more quickly and with less effort. Don't worry about the other parts of your goal. Just concentrate on completing the part that you are working on.

If your goal is to "write a best-selling novel," then the first step is to write an outline of the book. Don't worry about getting it right; just keep going. Think about each step you are taking as you are progressing towards the goal. If you are always thinking negatively, it can make you feel low. Always think of the best possible outcome, as this can help you achieve your goals.

Your attitude is a big part of your success. It can change your life and the way you see things.

CHAPTER 5

How to Think Like a Genius

Most of us aren't geniuses, but we do have the ability to think creatively. We all have genius within us. The difference is, most of us never use our creative genius. The first step to using your creative genius is to recognize it when you have it. You can do this by using the "Silly Putty" test. Silly Putty will stretch and then snap back to its original shape. When you become aware of a problem or an opportunity and you can see all the potential negative consequences of not taking action, you should mentally put some Silly Putty around those areas of your life. After a while, the Silly Putty will harden up and form a mental barrier around the area. This will cause you to pause and think before you automatically take action in that area. Once you do this enough, your brain will have formed a mental structure that will cause you to use your creative genius when you see a similar situation in the future.

How often do you use your creative genius? Not very often at all, because most of us never learn how to do it. We are so busy trying to be sensible and practical that we never stop to think outside the box. If we did, we might come up with a genius solution to a problem that has stumped everybody else for years. How can you use your creative genius without taking risks? The answer is simple: You simply find or create a "crowd" of people who have the same level of intelligence as you do (not necessarily the same level of experience). Find or create a group of people who have the same "mental Silly Putty" that you have around the parts of their lives where they are not taking risks. Next, tell those people about your genius idea. Ask them if they think it's worth a try. Listen to their feedback. Take their suggestions into consideration. Then, take a chance on your idea. If it doesn't work, at least you'll have learned something new that will help you in the future because there's nothing wrong in giving your idea a try. If it does work, you'll have created something new and wonderful that will make you rich and famous. I have given thousands of seminars over the past 20-years and this is the most important thing I have ever told my audiences. Most of you are not going to be rich and famous by doing what I say... but... you will dramatically increase your chances of success if you will simply allow yourself to occasionally use your creative genius to find or create a "crowd" of people who share your same level of intelligence and who have the same level of "mental Silly Putty" as you do.

There are only two kinds of people in this world: "Doers" and "Thought Stoppers." Those are the only two types of people you will ever meet. Everything else is a variation of those two basic types of people. Doers take actions. They get things done. They accomplish things. Those who don't do anything are just sitting around thinking about stuff. Thinking about nothing is not the same as been stop thinking. Instead, it is more like pondering. Pondering is like meditation for the brain. When you are pondering, your brain is occupied with re-evaluating information. It is sorting through data. Data is the stuff that thoughts are made of. Thoughts are data. Therefore, the process of pondering is making your brain work.

Pondering is not the same as thinking. Most people think they are pondering when in fact, they are merely thinking. You know the difference between pondering and thinking? It's simple: Thinkers ask questions while ponderers reevaluate the answers they already have. Here's an example: Let's say you have a thought such as "Gee, I wonder what Mozart would think about today's world?" Well, you are a thinker because you have just asked a question. However, if you were to say, "I wonder if Mozart would be surprised at all the things he couldn't accomplish in his life," then you are pondering. Pondering is a much more productive activity than thinking. Why? Because thinking takes time. Thinking is not like doing something; thinking is like looking at something. In other words, thinking is passive. You are merely observing something without taking any action. Pondering is different. You take an action. You get something done. Pondering is the opposite of thinking. It's just the opposite. Thinkers ponder and ponderers do. Those who don't do anything are the ones who are just sitting around thinking about stuff. Thinking about nothing is not the same as been stop thinking. Instead, it is more like pondering. When you are pondering, your brain is occupied with re-evaluating information.

To begin with, when you think of a problem as a mountain, A problem that seems unsolvable will seem

148

like a mountain that is too hard to climb. However, if you see the problem as a hill, it won't seem so difficult. Hills are easier to climb than mountains.

Now, once you see the problem as a hill, you need to start thinking about ways to scale the hill. The way to do this is to divide the hill into sections. Think of each section as a small hill. The first thing you should do is identify the easiest part of the hill to climb. The easiest part of a hill is usually at the top where there are no obstacles. Once you've identified the easiest part of the hill, you should focus on that area. Ask yourself what you can do to make it easier to get to the top. Can you cut some trees down? Build a retaining wall? Grout some steps? Lay some carpeting? Anything like that? The point is, once you've identified the easiest part of the hill, you should concentrate your efforts on making it easier to reach that part of the hill. After you've done that, you should ask yourself what else you can do to make it even easier. Maybe you can find some natural steps or maybe you can lay some concrete. Whatever. The idea is you keep dividing up the problem (the hill) until you have identified all the easiest parts of the hill. Now, once you've divided the problem up into sections, you need to think about ways to combine those sections into one big hill. This will make it much easier to scale the whole hill.

8 Techniques To Maximize Your Potential and Achieve Anything

We all have natural abilities that are hard-wired into our brains. These are called "mental processes". We all have them, no matter what people say about us. Some people are more skilled in certain mental processes than others. There is one particular mental process that I have identified as the key to all successful performance. This is a very valuable mental process, and it is especially important when we are trying to improve our performance. What this mental process is, is the ability to instantly create an "image" of how something should look, feel and sound. If you can do this, you will be able to visualize yourself performing better. If you can't do this, it will be extremely difficult for you to become a high-performing, top-level achiever. Here are 8 techniques to help you develop this mental process.

- Have goals

- Have a plan

- Do everything with your head

- Never give up

- Be positive

- Learn from your mistakes

- Do something every day

- Be a leader

Summary

Most of us have the ability to think creatively, but don't know how to use it. How can you use your creative genius without taking risks? Find or create a group of people who have the same level of intelligence as you and ask them for help. There are only two kinds of people in this world: "Doers" and "Thought Stoppers". Everything else is a variation of those two basic types of people.

Pondering is like meditation for the brain. Data is the stuff that thoughts are made of. Thoughts are data. Most people think they are pondering when in fact, they are merely thinking. Thinkers ask questions while ponderers reevaluate the answers they already have.

Pondering is a much more productive activity than thinking because it takes time. Thinking about nothing is not the same as been stop thinking. Identify the easiest part of a hill and then think about ways to make it easier to climb. We all have natural abilities that are hard-wired into our brains called "mental processes". Mental processes are the ability to create an "image" of how something should look, feel and sound.

Gratitude

I'd like to thank you for taking the time to read this book; I hope you found it useful. I'd appreciate your input on whether I succeeded or not, because it took me a great effort to make sure that this book is very useful and impactful to all my audience and readers. It would gladden my heart if you could leave a review on the product's retail page describing how this book has benefited you. Your feedback is really valuable to me, as I am eager to learn about your accomplishments. Nothing makes me happier than knowing that my work has helped someone achieve their goals and grow in life; it also motivates me to continue developing and better serving you, as well as encourage other readers to be positively influenced by my work. I value your input tremendously and will never take it for granted.

To share your success story, go to the product's retail page.

If your feedback is unfavourable, it is conceivable that you were not sufficiently impressed, or that you have a suggestion, error, recommendation, or criticism for us to address; we apologize for the inconvenience (remember, we are human, we are not perfect, and we are constantly striving to improve).

Rather than posting negative or dissatisfied feedback on this book's retail product page, please submit your feedback, suggestion, or complaint to

"Amoleypublishing@gmail.com" so that necessary corrections, improvements, and implementation can be made swiftly for a better reading experience.

Thank you again for taking the time to read this book. Have a nice day!

Recommended Books to Also Read:

I would also love to recommend some related books that may be of help to you or your loved ones below, check it out.

Event Planning Toolkit: Simplified Guide To Become A Successful Event Planner/Manager (Tips For Beginners And Seniors) getbook.at/Event-Planning-Toolkit

Acknowledgements

The Glory of this book success goes to God Almighty and my beautiful Family, Fans, Readers & well-wishers, Customers, and Friends for their endless support and encouragement.

About The Author

Amoo O. Olaleye is one of Africa's most sought-after investment and business coach and a notable event planner.

His first book, Event Planning Toolkit: Simplified Guide To Become A Successful Event Planner/Manager (Tips For Beginners And Seniors), has been so impactful for his readers.

He uses an integrative and more functional approach to his discipline, investments, and businesses. His primary motivation is to assist others in discovering their goals and dreams and becoming the person they aspire to be in their respective disciplines in order to create a well-rounded healthy lifestyle tailored to their individual needs to help them perform at their peak.

CPSIA information can be obtained
at www.ICGtesting.com
Printed in the USA
LVHW041809250322
714400LV00008B/835